Live Free or Croak

Live Free or Croak

Poems by

Larry Rogers

Golden Antelope Press
715 E. McPherson
Kirksville, Missouri 63501
2017

ISBN   978-1-936135-27-1 (1-936135-27-2)

Library of Congress Control Number: 2017935231

Published by:
Golden Antelope Press
715 E. McPherson
Kirksville, Missouri 63501

Available at:
Golden Antelope Press
715 E. McPherson
Kirksville, Missouri, 63501
Phone: (660) 665-0273
http://www.goldenantelope.com
Email: ndelmoni@gmail.com

Acknowledgments:

Some of these poems, often in earlier versions, were first published in the following journals. Grateful acknowledgement to the editors of these journals.

- *A Clean, Well-lighted Place.*
- *Abbey.*
- *The Chariton Review.*
- *Chiron Review.*
- *The Dead Mule School of Southern Literature.*
- *Hanging Loose.*
- *Kentucky Review.*
- *Nerve Cowboy.*
- *The New York Quarterly.*
- *Pearl.*
- *Rattle.*
- *Rusty Truck.*
- *Samisdat.*
- *The Sand Canyon Review.*
- *The San Pedro River Review.*
- *The Smudge.*
- *The South Carolina Review.*
- *Spitball.*
- *Sulpher River Poetry Review.*
- *Wormwood Review.*

For Judy

Contents

Live Free or Croak

First Loss of the Season

Prospect of robins
wedged into April,
a circle of celebration,
of spring & sun-stained
Johnson County peaches,
star of summers,
somewhere in the eastern sky.

While Mother is lowered
into loose black dirt,
Brother & I, 4 & 3,
forlorn wildflowers,
stare off toward
a distant ridge
where the Rock Island
is emerging from
a tunnel of pine.

Mr Rescue

When I forgot the words
to a song I could always
count on Bob for help.
It was like breaking down
on a musical highway
and calling Mr Rescue.
He would mouth the next line
and I wouldn't miss a beat.
For 20 years we railed in
harmony against the ruling class.
The joints we played weren't
the minor leagues of the music industry;
they were the sandlots.
What sparse crowds we did attract were
usually too drunk to appreciate
3-chord missiles fired at their masters.
Once in Dallas we asked
a club owner how much longer
he wanted us to play
and he actually said Until
the SWAT team arrives.
You should have died on a tiny stage,
Bob, not in a tiny apartment,
a reminder to call Affordable Dentures,
for a good reason to smile, tacked on
the wall you were found leaning against.
You should have died on a stage
behind the chicken wire that
protected us from our adoring fans
and which you rightly pointed out
also protected them from us.

She wanted

That voiceless boy
In the back
Of the classroom
The boy with
The battered past

She wanted
To make it all better
But he kept
Walking away
Before she could tell him
He kept walking away
Without a word

She wanted
To follow him
Step inside
His boarding house door
Establish her credentials
With these words:

The world says
The quiet ones
Are dangerous
I would remind the world
Of those who quietly
Give us poetry
Of those who quietly
Give us conscience

She liked speeches
Desperately wanted
To deliver this one

But she was a healer
Not a follower

And he kept
Walking away
Before she could tell him

He kept walking away
Without a word

Another Boy

I'm the neighborhood prowler
My feet aren't sore
But I'm taking a short vacation
Because of the unsporting way
I've been treated lately
Oh, I can tell by the giggling
    and gossiping
Some of you like discovering
Footprints outside your windows
But you're gonna have to
Turn off the flashlights
    and call off the dogs
Or find yourselves another boy

Another Cigarette

When I was twelve
pedaling home from
the post office
I passed a naked lady
sitting on a porch
smoking a cigarette.

She was 40ish, pretty,
and I recognized her
almost immediately as
the lady who worked
part-time behind
the soda fountain at
Stewart's Drug Store.

Of course, I circled
the block. But when I
came back around she
wasn't there. And she
wasn't there the next
500 times I circled
that block over the years.

And she was never again
behind the soda fountain
at Stewart's Drug Store, either.

Lines Written by a Desk Clerk Dressed in Black

She meets them
on the Internet
and they arrive
at odd hours.

One says he thumbed
from Salina to Joplin
and then walked
the last eighty miles.

When I ask
if he knows
she doesn't
have legs,
he steps outside
and lights up
an unlucky.

Which one's Melvin?
she barks from
her wheelchair
as she enters the lobby.

And when he races in
and raises his
trembling hand
she commands him
to follow her
into an elevator.

A burning desire
to meet
the Internet legend
they all say
when I ask
why they are here.

And when I ask
if they know
the Internet legend
has a poor
disposition
and neither arms
nor legs,

they step outside
and light up
unluckies,
or change the subject,
or turn sullen
and slander
the coffee I've made

from the finest beans
grown by Juan Valdez
on his plantation
in the most fertile
mountain valley
in all of the jittery
northern Andes.

Just Earth

The last time I saw Lonnie
he was shouting from an Ozark mountaintop:
This place is heaven on earth
to some people; it's just earth to me.

His rabbits had not multiplied;
a landslide had buried his marijuana patch.

The bitter laundry in his head
needed to be washed and hung out
to dry. But there was no washing machine
in his head and no clothesline.

Soon he would be moving on
deeper into these remote hills
trading his shack for a
sleeping bag under the sheltering pines
on the government land grab
that he still called home.

The Body That Is Never There

I don't like the story that says
every small town has its crazy.
I don't like it because in the small town
I grew up in the crazy was my father.
And I don't like it because its final chapter
is always entitled Heredity, or
Like Father Like Son, or Ditto.
I prefer stories about sane people
doing sane things: a father and son
fishing together, for example.
I don't like stories about fathers and sons
and Freud and psychoanalysis,
or stories about fathers and sons
and B.F. Skinner and behavioral mod.
And I certainly don't like stories
about fathers and sons and shock therapy.
Just tell me they're going fishing together.
Don't tell me on the way they decide
every bump in the road is human
and go back every time one is hit
to pick up the body that is never there.

The Card Players

He said Let's play Crazy Uncle.
I did not know the game but said OK.
He said Mine felt betrayed
both by those who opposed the war
and by those who supported it:
didn't want a homecoming parade
but complained when one wasn't given;
tossed his Good Conduct Medal
into a dumpster behind Jim's Barbershop
then crawled in to reclaim it.
When Jim said You appear to be conflicted,
he took offense and swore off haircuts forever.
I said I'll see your crazy uncle
and raise you a crazy aunt.
Mine was always on his way
to sunny California; got as far as Sallisaw once,
on a motorcycle with a sidecar
in which my crazy aunt fit quite nicely.
Well, he said, that's not
how the game is played.
I did not know how to play that game
and I did not know how to play the next game,
Celestial Poker, which I won as well,
by simply letting the stars fall where they may.

Strumming

One morning
we received
a call from
a young lieutenant
who said he
and his radio operator
were pinned down
and could not
hold out much longer.

Later that day,
we found the radioman;
what had been
done to him
was unspeakable.

We never found
the young lieutenant
whose east Texas
piney woods twang
sounded like
a flattop guitar
with an untuned
bottom string.

Security Farm

At midnight in a mountain hamlet
I board a train called
The Asian Empress. It's practically
a toy. Something from a Six Flags
amusement park. As it chugs off
into the mist, I recall planting,
30 years ago in this very province,
a row of spies beside a row of counterspies
on what I called a security farm.

There was a girl with pink skin,
a peach in every pore, doing
a little dance in the mud. She asked,
"Why don't you call your crops
by their real names?" And I pointed to
a water buffalo that wasn't really
a water buffalo in a rice paddy that wasn't
really a rice paddy and said, "Georgia,
you already know too much."

Sipping a Bud in the He's Not Here Club

It made the cowboys nervous
when the cowgirls began
dancing with each other;

there were so many cowboys
willing and available.

When the cowgirls persisted
the cowboys became morose.

Even today many sit bitterly alone
or simply dumbfounded

in dimly-lit roadhouses.

Roni

At 17,
She fronted
A band called
Musical Malpractice
She and her voice
Were rough around
The edges like
Every Sonic burger
Ever served
I liked her
Imperfection in
An imperfect world
Makes perfect sense
I always told her
Don't practice
You might
Get it right
And ruin everything

Noodle Soup

The beautiful
and experienced
Mary Gardner
was my first date ever.
I was 16; she
was 2 years older.
I was like a guy
who has never
even seen a
baseball game
playing in one
at the major
league level.
After a movie
she suggested
we drive over to
The Finger Bowl.
I didn't know
what she was
talking about—
The Finger Bowl
being a euphemism
for a secluded,
makeout spot
only the more
experienced local
kids frequented—
and while Mary
looked on incredulously
I drove around for
what seemed like hours
looking for a
Chinese restaurant.

One day,

after 20 years
of less than
marital bliss,
Harry looked
at his wife
and said: Who
are you, anyway?

A fair question, she replied.
Why, I'm the Belle of
the Hippie Ball. Remember
my long blonde hair
and my disdain for
shoes or sandals.
I accompanied you
to a basketball game
on a snowy December
night 20 years ago.
I was barefooted and
you asked me to marry you.
Those days, you used
to say: All you have
to do is get naked
and walk toward me
and all my philosophy
and poetry go right out
the proverbial window.
This is who I am. Darling.

Harry calmly walked
outside, got in
his BMW and drove
as fast as possible
into the nearest
concrete embankment.

At his funeral
there were no

barefooted ladies
but several middle-
aged men with
long hair.

How We'll Know Fats Is Back

One night in a Minnesota bar
an old man will begin talking.

When his story
requires specifics
a beer will help.

When a listener
shouts Imposter
a bouncer will help.

When he's done
he'll pull a little bag
from his secret pocket
and sprinkle its contents
on a pool table

whose pockets will instantly
become wider than before.

We Miss You

You were riding shotgun
in a chopper that crashed
after clipping a palm tree
at 95 mph and walked away.
Back in the States, you
were behind the wheel of a
Dodge Charger struck head-on
by a dump truck driven by
a 16-year-old diabetic under
the influence of 2 chocolate milkshakes
and walked away. Living such
a charmed life, you must have thought
death could not touch you.
Why else would you have ignored
the lump on your testicle,
the cough that would not go away,
and joked about having slept
in puddles of Agent Orange?
You left us much too soon and knowing
you could have prevented that
is frustrating. Every year on
the anniversary of your death your pals
gather at your grave and smash
a whiskey bottle on your tombstone.
Monroe says he would like to smash it
on your skull but he's no grave robber.

Monsoon Sky

In high school
I read a book
about submariners.
Anxiety, its
author said,
is sweating out
depth charges.
Then I couldn't
imagine a fear
so intense;
this morning
that's easy
on this hill
with a number
for its name.
Every bunker
and every hole
in the ground
in which two
or more grunts
are gathered
is a little
mental hygiene clinic,
and it's still
impossible to manage
the stress here.
Bloated corpses
litter the landscape,
and choppers, at
max capacity with
our wounded, splash
like giant tadpoles
across the monsoon sky.

Lily

She is 3,
balanced
doe-like
against my hip.
What shall I do
with her?
Prepare her
for things that bite
or buy her
another dozen
purple balloons?

A Horse-Drawn Cart with Car Tires for Wheels

In June of 1967 two local boys
died in Southeast Asia.
A few days later I saw
a horse-drawn cart, with
car tires for wheels, carrying
two grieving, teenage girls
to a tiny cemetery that
was another two miles down
the dusty path they were on.
In better times I would
have good-naturedly derided
their mode of transportation.
But this morning I just
pulled over and let them pass.
In San Francisco and other
faraway places, it might
have been a summer of love,
but in the Hillbilly Outback
I recall it being a summer
of nineteen-year-old widows.

Howdy Neighbor

Don't be alarmed
if some midnight
you hear a howling
in your cornfield
that sounds like
Johnny Rotten covering
a Glenn Miller tune
on a sinking ocean liner.
It's just the Wolf Boy
welcoming you into
the piney woods of
west central Arkansas.
What did you expect,
a Walmart greeter?
60 miles from
the nearest town,
you dig a hole
in the ground,
cover it with a tin roof
and sandbags,
and call it a home.
Did you expect
a basket of fruit
from your only neighbor,
the meth dealer
who lives a mile
down the road?
This is a country
of unwise owls.
Among the animals
and people living here
only the animals
have good teeth.
You knew all this
and moved here anyway.
Don't be afraid. That howling in
your cornfield is just

the Wolf Boy
saying Hello.

Live Free or Croak

A sanctuary for moonshiners, marijuana growers, and merry pranksters, Frogtown's a tiny community in the piney woods of west central Arkansas.

There's one saloon in town and it's sundown when Hawkins Rogers bursts thru its ancient swinging doors.

It has been a long day and Hawk is thirsty.

The joint has a pool table, a jukebox, a dozen bar stools, and five red vinyl booths. The shuffleboard table has been removed to allow more space for dancing and fighting.

It's so dark inside that at first Hawkins doesn't recognize Ruby Canada sitting on a bar stool next to him.

Ruby is a bit of a recluse. Hawk can't remember the last time he's seen her in town. "Ruby, I'll be darned, where've you been?" Hawk says.

"Staying as far away from trouble like you as I can," Ruby half-smiles.

Everyone knows Ruby in the Frogtown area. But no one knows her well. Hawk knows her better than most.

They had gone to bed together a few years back. It hadn't meant anything to either of them. Both just thought it a friendly gesture on the other's part.

From that night and from other less intimate times being around her, Hawk has learned: Ruby is squeaky clean in some ways and dirty as bus depots in others. She takes milk to market on a horse-drawn cart with car tires for wheels. Soda pop has discolored her teeth but hasn't spoiled her smile. Her eyes are the color of the sky on one of those days in her childhood when she didn't get her way. Sometimes a crow flies over one of those days and she pauses to enjoy its wings.

At least this is how Hawk saw her several years ago. He jotted down these lines about her in a journal he was keeping then. He's thinking about that now when Ruby says, "Let's move to a booth. I have a dirty little secret and I'm dying to share it."

Hawk stands and picks up their glasses and they relocate.

"I terminated it."

"Terminated what?"

"Our baby. We made a baby that night, Hawkins."

Hawk can't tell whether Ruby is playing with him or not.

"This isn't funny, Ruby."

"I agree."

"You don't appear to be too upset about it."

"It was 10 years ago, Hawk."

"And you're just now telling me? Why now?"

"I just think you have the right to know."

"Damn straight I do."

"Anyway, now that I'm dying, what does it matter?"

"You're dying?"

"Pancreatic cancer. Doc Bailey says I might have 6 months."

Hawkins stares at the sign above the jukebox that reads Live Free or Croak. He looks at Ruby and says, "You look great."

"Thanks," Ruby says. "It's funny, I've never felt better."

"You still writing?" Ruby asks.

Hawk doesn't hear the question. He's studying Ruby and wondering if what people say about heredity is true.

Ruby's father and grandfather both required shock therapy.

"Every small town has its crazies and they're ours," Hawk remembers his mother saying.

But Ruby has never seemed crazy in a clinical way.

"I'm talked out," Ruby says, rising from her spot in the booth.

"You going?" Hawk asks.

"Yeah," Ruby says.

"Don't give up," Hawk says. "Doctors have been wrong before."

"I'm not giving up."

Hawk steps outside with her.

"What's next?"

"I'm going to see a fortune teller."

"Why?" Hawk asks.

"To get a second opinion," Ruby says over her shoulder.

Animal Crackers

My friend Pat Sullivan
didn't like animal crackers
but he liked biting
their heads off to show
how tough he was.
My sister didn't like
animal crackers either
but she liked the little
boxes they came in,
with a string on top;
she carried them around
like they were purses.
I didn't like how the wild animals
were pictured in cages on those boxes.
Elephants and tigers
should be left in their natural habitat.
But I liked the animal
crackers themselves.
And with those my sister didn't eat
and those decapitated ones
Pat Sullivan didn't eat,
I dined on animal crackers
like the high and mighty
dine on steak.

Spring

A stripper has moved
into the neighborhood.

Every day she walks
around the block,
always stopping
to discuss gardening
with my wife.

A beautiful redhead,
she lives quietly:
suns on her patio
and washes her Cadillac
every three days.

Today when she passed by
I was shaving my winter beard.

She watched it fall
on the carport.

Mixed with
mud and straw,
I told her,
an old man's beard
makes a fine
bird's nest.

And before day's end,
two industrious robins
had swooped down
and claimed
the little pile
of silver.

Once

we imbibed
a little concoction
rumored to be
something the Vietnamese
substituted for
embalming fluid:
part alcohol
and part who-knows-what.

Just enough alcohol
to lift our spirits
and/or numb
our hearts and minds,
and not quite enough
who-knows-what
to kill us.

Delta Town

I stand under
a streetlamp,
collar turned up
against the wind
that isn't blowing,
conversing with myself
in a whisper
perfected while homeless
and hanging out
in a public library.

Across the street
swinging doors open
in a one hundred
year old saloon
like dark curtains
being parted in
a condemned building
by dark children
who still live there.

Probation

Trading one
Addiction
For another
I'll watch
Too much TV

When a court-appointed
Witch doctor
Checking out
My cognitive state
Asks my name
I'll say I'll be right back
After these messages

When he condescendingly replies
That's an unusual name
I'll say OK Repairman
Call me Technical Difficulties

Or I'll just sneak over
To Sugarloaf Lake
Soak up some rays
And show off
My ankle monitor

Reading Too Much

This morning at breakfast,
Hank, age 4, describes
his new pal, the little
girl next door: Curly hair
and real big thumbs.
Later, at work, Harley sweeps
in, says: You read too much.
That's why you don't
have 20-20 division.
A gal in Greenwood died
because she read too much.
That doesn't sound right, I protest.
Maybe she had a brain
tumor or something.
Brain tumors don't
necessarily kill you, he says.
2 years ago, his niece
had a 26 pound brain tumor
removed from her belly.
Now, 3 nights a week,
she dances in a cage
at The Pottawatomie Club.

He leaves to look
for a dustpan.
I step outside
to air out
my brainpan.

Either I'm
seeing things
or a hearse
is rolling
down Main
followed by
a bookmobile.

The Farmer's Bank of Greenwood

Dear Sirs:
I would like to borrow
5,000 dollars.
I have as collateral
24 unpublished poems.
I also have a picture
of Don The Blazer Blasingame
sliding into second in his last summer
with the Redbirds.

Furthermore, Sirs,
regarding the 200 dollars
I borrowed here several years ago ...
Be advised that with the granting of this loan
I shall begin payments on that other
at once.

The Mule

There is a way
you sing
when you finally realize
you will never be
the world's greatest singer,
nor the world's
greatest songwriter,
nor the world's greatest
jump shooter,
nor the world's greatest
anything.

You are 33 before
you finally begin
braying from your heart.

Pace in Our Time (1979)

Overheard as I was punching in:
They put in a peacemaker
to fix my old man's heart;
I've never seen the old feller
as paceful as he is now.

So begins another shift
at Duplex Manufacturing.
Assembly line workers shape,
shine and ship toolboxes here.

Through a grimy window
I see the green hills
and valleys of western Arkansas
whose beauty my father
so admired he once said:
A man is lucky to be
part of this postcard.

He didn't say this is the only postcard
and he didn't say a man
couldn't be luckier someplace else.

And perhaps I should have
migrated with cousins
and classmates to California's
factories and farms.

But I stayed and today
find myself asking the son of
a man with a broken heart
if that peacemaker is a Begin or Sadat.

Caregiving

I have a healthy
year old son
& a 70 year old
mother with Alzheimer's.

He's learning
how to speak;
she's forgotten how.

From the kitchen
I see him
telling her something;
she isn't listening.

Dinner is served:
he's learning
how to chew;
she's forgotten how
to swallow.

I spoon feed him;
tube feed her.

Rock him
to sleep,
carry him
to bed.

Come back
& rock her.

Sherman

Remember that boy in the back
of the classroom so timid even saying
present when the roll was called
required taking a deep breath
and holding it for 20 seconds before
slowly exhaling to pacify his
palpitating heart? He grew up in the most
anti-social clan in the Hillbilly Outback.
On the remote hill they called home, dust
kicking up from what passed for a road,
a car or truck could be seen approaching
from miles away. Outsiders, someone would
shout, and they would all scatter
into the woods until their uninvited
guests departed. 62 now, his yard
hasn't been mowed in years or since
he last spoke to neighbors and trimmed
his 2-inch long fingernails. From
his crumbling porch he stares at ceramic
deer munching concrete in an industrial
park, ready to bolt for the weeds behind
his shack if anyone stops to say hello.

The Pine Cross

I grew up
in west
central
Arkansas

I called it
the Hillbilly Outback

It was just
cow flop
and crazy people

I had a pal
called Moonshine

I had a pal
called Meth

Unless you
count time
spent at
the pig farm
in Grady
none of us
ever got out

When I was
a child
deep in
a bruised forest
I found
a pine cross
that had
been used
by hunters
for target
practice

and managed

with great
difficulty to
get it home—

just as Mama
was slamming
the door on
a Jehovah's Witness

A pine cross
has magical power
and I decided
to lean this one
against our
front gate
to ward off
salesmen who
before moving on
down the road
were stomping on
Mama's unwelcome mat
to get her dirt
off their shoes

Stray

I sympathize with the kid.
Nipples were all his mother ever gave him;
his old man gave him less.

For Andy Who Signed with the San Francisco Giants in 1972 (Written After Finding His Bubble Gum Card Contract in the Smokehouse)

He wanted his ashes spread
over a pasture in Logan County
that decades earlier had been
a ballfield on which the Dean brothers,
Dizzy and Daffy, had played
when they were boys.

When he was a boy
wanting to get away
from the worries of this world,
he would go there
and commune with
their carefree spirits.

Accommodating him
one bright, April morning
I did not hear the pop
of a fastball shooting
into the heart of a catcher's mitt,
or early 20th century
infield chatter,
only my own unsteady voice
giving the barefooted Diz
a glowing scouting report
on another local boy.

Wringing Out the Mops

There are days you
don't want to see
your reflection in
the floor. But you
polish hard until it's
mirror-like anyway.

There's a little art
in anything done well.
This floor is a canvas.
Don't laugh; sometimes
art is simply caring in
a way no one else does.

When Marlon Perkins died I heard

a woman say I would rather the chimps
had captured him, had tagged him,
and driven his collaborator, Jim Fowler,
to higher ground. And wouldn't it
have been lovely, this normally taciturn
lady continued, if Marlon had been
held captive until he forgot how
to hold a spoon, forgot how to chew and swallow,
forgot how to breathe. And then, just
before his final gasp, had been nursed to
full strength and released in the heart of
his beloved wild kingdom with a radio
transmitter attached to his balls so
the primates could study his mating habits.

Last Dance

Given the vastness
of the universe,
rock and roll's a
pretty small explosion.

But here we are,
the Greenwood High School
graduating class of 1965,
still a few happy months
from our ranks being thinned
by car wrecks and Nam,
shakin' all over.

For Mrs Rogers

At 65, I'm still bringing apples
with bites taken out of them
to a kindergarten teacher, the one
I married 33 years ago; and she
is still having to remind me
not to resent authority so much
and not to play so rough with others.

Lifers

A drill sergeant returns home from
another day of war games. Real blood's
fresh upon his green clothing. A boy
snaps to attention, salutes dutifully.
This pleases the drill sergeant. He
swings the boy around the room. He stumbles
and they fall, together. The boy doesn't
like the drill sergeant: he drinks too much
to help with long division. And it's a
damn lie: his story about going straight
from the 6th grade to the Big Red One
and returning from Nam with a Bronze Star
and Purple Heart pinned to his bare chest.
The refrigerator is full of beer. When
the drill sergeant finishes one, it's
the boy's duty to bring him another. The boy
soldiers on until the drill sergeant
passes out at which time he covers him
with a blanket and sets his clock for 4 AM.
It's the least a boy can do for his country.

The Dying Room

Uncle Carl said when he was
rolled into the dying room
his biggest fear was being
mistaken for dead and buried alive.
It took all his remaining strength
to wiggle the little finger on
his left hand and then he worried
that no one noticed. But
someone did and he was
rolled from that makeshift morgue
to a makeshift aid station,
and following 18 months in
VA hospitals he returned
to civilian life playing sax
in a Hot Springs jazz club
where he met and married a
pretty hat check girl whom
he called his satin doll, the name
of the Duke Ellington classic that
Aunt Cora said he often played for her
in their little cabin in the piney woods
of west central Arkansas.

Dueling Phobias

He showered 12 times daily
but didn't feel clean until
he scrubbed his flesh away.

For someone who hates attention,
he certainly stands out.

Rain

"B" battery is pulling out from Quang Tri City and moving to Hue where the battle for that city is still raging.

When PFC Hawkins Rogers hears two guys are being left behind to guard a broken down half-track, he knows he will be Captain Walker's first choice.

The captain and Rogers have been at odds since the old man overheard Rogers calling him a coward for repeatedly volunteering the battery for dangerous missions that did not require his presence.

The second man chosen is Sergeant Red, a notorious alcoholic.

Being left behind will be a very dicey proposition. Every other friendly unit in the area, including the 101st Airborne, has already left. Rogers and Red will be alone, miles from help if they need it.

A gun bunny takes pity on them and gives Red a quart of whiskey. "Hope it helps you guys forget how dangerous this assignment is," the gun bunny says.

The gun bunny is full of good news: "There's a company of North Vietnamese just over that rise," he adds, pointing south to a steep ridge on the other side of a deep valley.

Two pals stop by and offer their condolences to Hawk. It's a joke without a punchline. Both know their buddy's in danger and both are deeply worried about him.

Before the last vehicle in the battery has disappeared from sight, Red has already gulped down a half pint of whiskey.

Rogers and Red have taken shelter in a ten foot long and five foot deep hole in the ground. It has a tin roof covered by a few sandbags.

As darkness falls Red continues his assault on sobriety.

There's no conversing with Red. He's too hammered. So Rogers just stares out from an opening in the shelter, focusing on the valley and steep hill to his south.

"I don't see a damn thing," Rogers finally says, breaking the silence and turning around to look at Sergeant Red.

But Red doesn't hear Rogers. The sergeant has blacked out. The whiskey bottle, still in his right hand, is nearly empty.

Around midnight Rogers hears a sound coming from the south that can't be more than a hundred yards away. "Just my luck," Rogers whispers to himself. "Jesus."

Rogers climbs out from the hole in the ground and crawls to a spot a few yards behind it. From here it's easier to scan the south and southeast. Hearing and seeing nothing, Rogers crawls farther up the hill until he's at least a hundred yards from Red's position.

The valley is shrouded in fog. On the hill where Rogers lies a light mist is falling. Rogers stays in this position for over an hour without hearing or seeing anything that worries him.

Then squinting his eyes Rogers sees nine or ten figures emerging from the dense fog about 50 yards below him. Rogers doesn't want to believe what he's seeing. And these figures are moving up the hill toward Red. A squad of NVA, Rogers thinks. But are they really headed in Red's direction. Rogers isn't sure. At this point, he isn't even sure of his own location. And then Rogers hears the sound of boots moving up another hill about 50 yards off in another direction. More NVA. Jesus Jesus Jesus!!! Startled, Rogers struggles to remain calm.

Rogers is carrying a radio but using it now would give his position away.

Rogers doesn't move and breathes as quietly as possible. A cough would be fatal. Hell, a sigh would be fatal.

Rogers doesn't move until an hour after hearing the NVA go. Then he works his way back to where he left the sergeant and cautiously lowers himself into their little shelter.

Sergeant Red isn't there!

"Where the hell are you?" Rogers asks repeatedly and much too loudly. "WHERE THE HELL ARE YOU?"

The only thing he can do now is radio the battery in Hue. "A platoon from the 101st will pick you up at daybreak," Rogers is told.

Rogers can't believe any of this is really happening. Exhausted, he sits down on the mud floor of the shelter, his eyes transfixed on the spot where Sergeant Red had been lying. A few minutes later Rogers crawls over and takes a look outside.

A soft rain is falling all over the world.

CPSIA information can be obtained
at www.ICGtesting.com
Printed in the USA
FSOW02n1532150417
33051FS